ARABIAN HORSES

Lorijo Metz

PowerKiDS
press

New York

For Melissa Matson and her first horse, Pete

Published in 2013 by The Rosen Publishing Group, Inc.
29 East 21st Street, New York, NY 10010

Editor: Amelie von Zumbusch
Book Design: Kate Laczynski

Photo Credits: Back cover graphic (big horsehoe) © www.istockphoto.com/Deborah Cheramie; Back cover graphic (background horseshoes), c-over, pp. 6, 8, 9 (bottom), 12, 17, 20, 21, 22 Shutterstock.com; pp. 4, 5, 13 iStockphoto.com/Thinkstock; p. 7 © age fotostock/SuperStock; p. 9 (top) © www.istockphoto.com/Hanne Bratholm; p. 10 © www.istockphoto.com/Geoff Kuchera; p. 11 © Prenzel, Fritz/Animals Animals - Earth Scenes; p. 14 Niels van Gijn/AWL Images/Getty Images; p. 15 Abraham Cooper/The Bridgeman Art Library/ Getty Images; p. 16 Hulton Archive/Stringer/Getty Images; pp. 18—19 © www.istockphoto.com/Julie Vader.

Library of Congress Cataloging-in-Publication Data

Metz, Lorijo.
 Arabian horses / by Lorijo Metz. — 1st ed.
     p. cm. — (The world of horses)
 ISBN 978-1-4488-7426-2 (library binding) — ISBN 978-1-4488-7499-6 (pbk.) —
 ISBN 978-1-4488-7573-3 (6-pack)
 1. Arabian horse—Juvenile literature. I. Title.
 SF293.A8M48 2013
 636.1'12—dc23

                              2011045704

Manufactured in China

CPSIA Compliance Information: Batch #WKTS12PK: For Further Information contact Rosen Publishing, New York, New York at 1-800-237-9932

Contents

Arabians

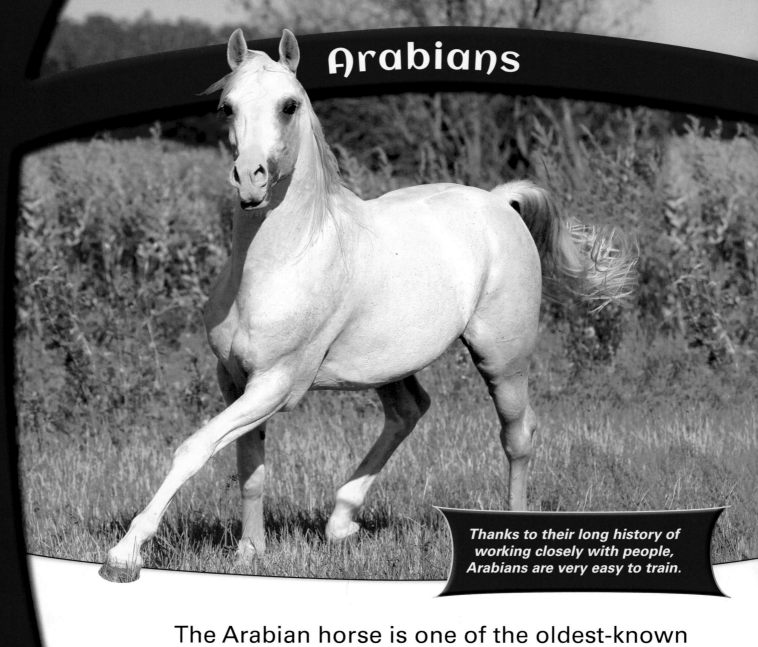

Thanks to their long history of working closely with people, Arabians are very easy to train.

The Arabian horse is one of the oldest-known **breeds**, or types, of horses. The Bedouins first raised these graceful horses. The Bedouins are a people who live in the deserts of the Middle East. Scientists think that the Bedouins

may have started raising Arabian horses almost 5,000 years ago.

Arabian horses now live in many parts of the world. Known for their beauty and speed, Arabians are one of the 10 most popular breeds of horses. They are also famous for winning long-distance races, like the Pan American **Endurance** Championships. Most important, they are good with people.

Gentle, Hot-Blooded Horses

Life in the desert where Arabians began was hard. Days were hot and nights were cold. Food and water was hard to find. Arabians and humans learned to depend on each other. While Arabians helped people cross the hot desert sands, people made sure their horses had plenty

A healthy Arabian horse will live for between 20 and 30 years.

Arabian horses often play with each other. Trainers teach these strong animals not to play with people in ways that could hurt them.

of food and water. This special bond between Arabian horses and people continues today.

While Arabians are gentle and loving, you may often hear them called hot-blooded. This is because Arabians are lively and fast. However, they are also smart and easy to train. When trained right, Arabian horses are easy to work with.

Most Arabians are solid colors such as gray, brown, and chestnut. Chestnut horses have reddish-brown coats, manes, and tails. Some Arabians are bay, or reddish brown with a black mane, tail, and legs.

Arabians have small, pointed ears and large, dark eyes. Like upside-down triangles, their heads narrow to small noses and mouths, or

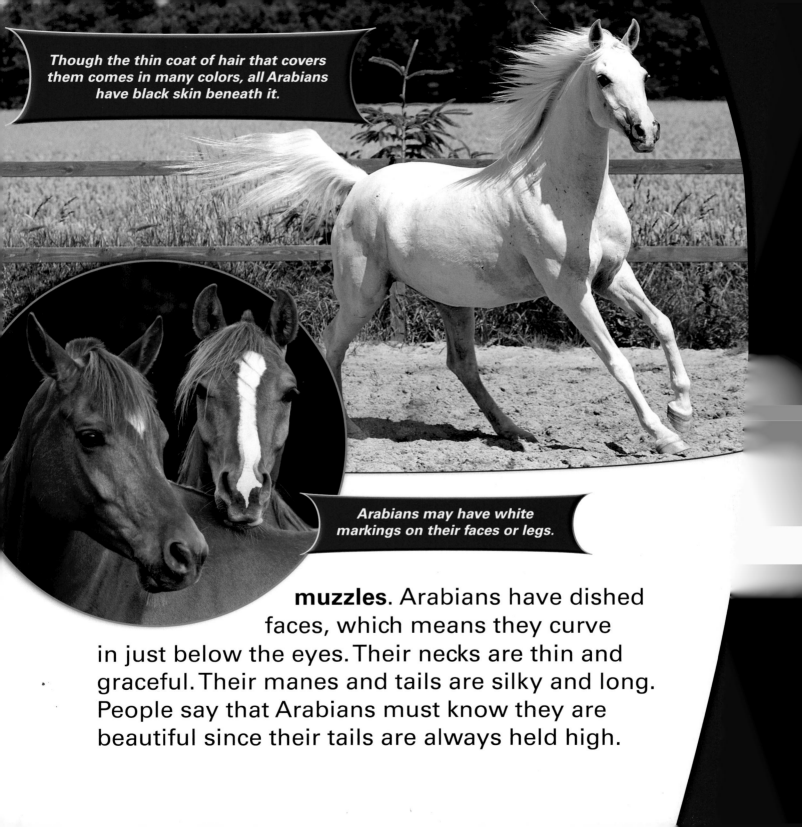

Though the thin coat of hair that covers them comes in many colors, all Arabians have black skin beneath it.

Arabians may have white markings on their faces or legs.

muzzles. Arabians have dished faces, which means they curve in just below the eyes. Their necks are thin and graceful. Their manes and tails are silky and long. People say that Arabians must know they are beautiful since their tails are always held high.

Arabian horses need plenty of open land for exercise. They also need housing, such as a barn or **stable**, with their own **stalls** filled with clean straw to sleep in. Daily brushing is important to keep their coats and skin clean. A visit once a year from a **veterinarian**, or animal doctor, is also very important.

Though years of desert living made Arabian horses able to survive on less, they still need plenty of fresh food

Arabians that get ridden a lot need to eat more food than Arabians that lead less active lives.

This girl is feeding hay to a young Arabian horse.

and water. Arabians eat hay and alfalfa. When working hard, they also eat oats, barley, and other grains. To replace salt lost from sweating, they need blocks of salt to lick.

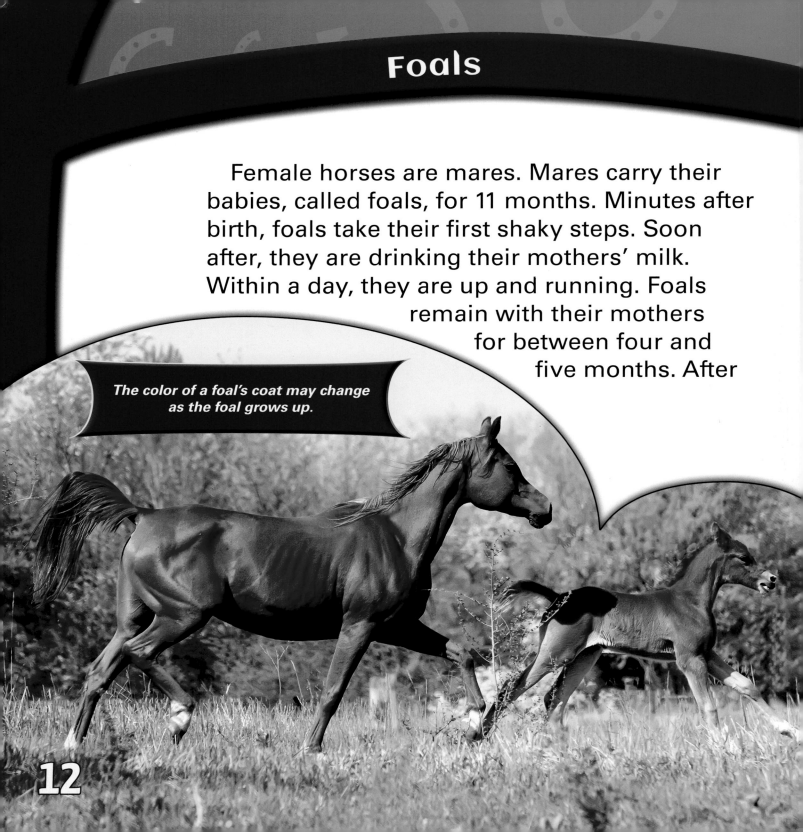

Foals

Female horses are mares. Mares carry their babies, called foals, for 11 months. Minutes after birth, foals take their first shaky steps. Soon after, they are drinking their mothers' milk. Within a day, they are up and running. Foals remain with their mothers for between four and five months. After

The color of a foal's coat may change as the foal grows up.

that, they spend most of their time with other young horses.

Horses are measured in **hands**. One hand equals 4 inches (10 cm). Arabian horses grow to be from 14 to 15 hands high. They are measured from the ground to the tops of their **withers**, or shoulders.

Arabians in the Desert

Arabian horses come from a part of the Middle East known as the Arabian Peninsula. The Bedouins who raised them lived in tribes. They also raised animals such as goats and sheep. Bedouins moved around the desert so that their animals could find plants to eat. They lived in tents.

The deserts of the Arabian Peninsula are beautiful, but they are also a hard place to live.

This painting from 1860 shows two Bedouins with an Arabian horse.

The Bedouins were often at war. They needed horses that were fast and strong. Arabian horses could cover long distances with little water.

Bedouins prized their horses, even sharing their tents with them. This was good for the horses and good for the Bedouins. If a stranger approached, the horses would stamp their hooves in warning.

The Godolphin Arabian was a famous Arabian owned by the Earl of Godolphin. He is one of three Arabian horses that helped found the Thoroughbred, an English horse breed.

In the past, people used horses in wars. Most warhorses were strong, but Arabian horses were both strong and fast. Once people from Europe, Asia, and America saw these horses, they wanted them. Arabian horses were often **bred** with other types of horses. Many breeds of horses have some Arabian blood.

People other than Bedouins began raising Arabian horses, too. In 1881, Wilfrid Scawen Blunt and Anne Blunt brought Arabians to their home in Crabbet Park, England. They feared **purebred** Arabian horses, or Arabian horses that were not mixed with other breeds, might die out. Crabbet Arabians are still prized by people all over the world.

This horse is a quarter horse. Arabians were one of the horses that people used to shape this American horse breed.

Arabian Horses Today

Arabian horses now live in many parts of the world, from Australia and Spain to North America and South America. Today, these horses are no longer used for war. Many people own and ride Arabians simply because they are beautiful.

Years of living in deserts have made Arabians perfect for long-distance rides. People also ride Arabian horses when hunting or trail riding. With their long, silky manes and tails held high, you also often see these horses in parades. Finally, their gentle way with people has made them popular in programs for people with **disabilities**.

This girl is taking a riding lesson on an Arabian. Since Arabians tend to be gentle, they are good horses for people who are just learning how to ride.

19

Arabians are the stars of long-distance horse racing, known as endurance racing. One of the oldest endurance races is the Tevis Cup. Covering 100 miles (161 km) through the Sierra Nevada in California, it is one of the hardest endurance races. Since this race began, all but two of the winners have been part or purebred Arabians.

Arabians are also popular show horses. In horse

In some horse shows, Arabians also compete in costume classes. In these, the horse and its rider are dressed in costumes.

The Tevis Cup's official name is the Western States Trail Ride. It passes through the Sierra Nevada, seen here.

shows, Arabians **compete**, or go up against, other horses in classes. The halter class is like a beauty contest. Horses are judged by how they look. In the dressage class, horses must accomplish special riding moves.

Today, Arabian horses and people work together in many ways. In **equine therapy**, therapists use horses, such as Arabians, to help people overcome problems. Arabian horses even act in movies! In 1979, an Arabian named Cass Ole starred in the movie *The Black Stallion*. Many people wanted to own Arabians after seeing him. Whether racing across deserts or starring in movies, Arabian horses and people will always have a special bond.

Glossary

bred (BRED) To have brought a male and a female animal together so they will have babies.

breeds (BREEDZ) Groups of animals that look alike and have the same relatives.

compete (kum-PEET) To go against another in a game or contest.

disabilities (dis-uh-BIH-luh-teez) Conditions such as blindness that make people unable to do certain things.

endurance (en-DUR-ints) Strength and the ability to go long distances without getting tired easily.

equine therapy (EE-kwyn THER-uh-pee) Using horses to treat people's problems.

hands (HANDZ) A measurement for the height of a horse. One hand is equal to 4 inches (10 cm), about the width of an adult human hand.

muzzles (MUH-zelz) The parts of animals' heads that come forward and include the nose.

purebred (PYUHR-bred) Animals that are only of one breed.

stable (STAY-bul) A building in which farm animals are kept and fed.

stalls (STOLZ) Spots for animals in a barn or stable.

veterinarian (veh-tuh-ruh-NER-ee-un) A doctor who treats animals.

withers (WIH-therz) A place between the shoulders of a dog or horse.

Index

Websites

Due to the changing nature of Internet links, PowerKids Press has developed an online list of websites related to the subject of this book. This site is updated regularly. Please use this link to access the list:
www.powerkidslinks.com/woh/arab/